Epic Cars

Challenger SRT Hellcat

JULIA GARSTECKI

BLACK RABBIT BOOKS

Bolt is published by Black Rabbit Books
P.O. Box 3263, Mankato, Minnesota, 56002.
www.blackrabbitbooks.com

Marysa Storm, editor; Catherine Cates, interior designer; Grant Gould, cover designer; Omay Ayres, photo researcher

Library of Congress Cataloging-in-Publication Data
Names: Garstecki, Julia, author.
Title: Challenger SRT Hellcat / by Julia Garstecki.
Description: Mankato, Minnesota : Black Rabbit Books, [2020] | Series: Bolt. Epic cars | Includes index. | Audience: Ages 9-12. | Audience: Grades 4 to 6.
Identifiers: LCCN 2018015186 (print) | LCCN 2018016496 (ebook) | ISBN 9781680728439 (e-book) | ISBN 9781680728354 (library binding) | ISBN 9781644660348 (paperback)
Subjects: LCSH: Challenger automobile–Juvenile literature.
Classification: LCC TL215.C44 (ebook) | LCC TL215.C44 G37 2020 (print) | DDC 629.222/2–dc23
LC record available at https://lccn.loc.gov/2018015186

Special thanks to Justin Storm for his help with this book.

Printed in the United States. 1/19

Image Credits

ablog.dodge.com: DC SRT, 17 (top); chrysler-club.net: FocalNicko, 17 (btm), 32; dodge.com: FCA US, 8–9; Dreamstime: Raytags, 6; media.fcanorthamerica.com: Cover (car), 1, 3, 4–5, 11, 12, 13, 15, 16, 16–17, 18–19, 21, 22–23, 25, 26, 26–27, 28–29; Shutterstock: Elenamiv, Cover (bkgd); GarikProst, 21 (top right); Jan.Melichar, 31
Every effort has been made to contact copyright holders for material reproduced in this book. Any omissions will be rectified in subsequent printings if notice is given to the publisher.

Contents

CHAPTER 1

Racing Down the Road

The Dodge Challenger SRT Hellcat races down the street. It rumbles and roars. The **hulking** car looks like it eats other cars for breakfast. It rules the drag strip. Few cars can match its power.

SRT stands for Street and Racing Technology.

SRT

COMPARING HORSEPOWER OF MODERN CHALLENGERS

2018 SRT Demon

2018 SRT Hellcat

2018 SRT 392

2018 R/T Shaker

horsepower

Becoming a Beast

Dodge made the first Challengers from 1970 to 1974. In 2008, it started making the **muscle car** again. In 2014, the company introduced the Hellcat variation. No car had ever been built like it. The massive car had 707 **horsepower**. Dodge has since continued to make new Challengers.

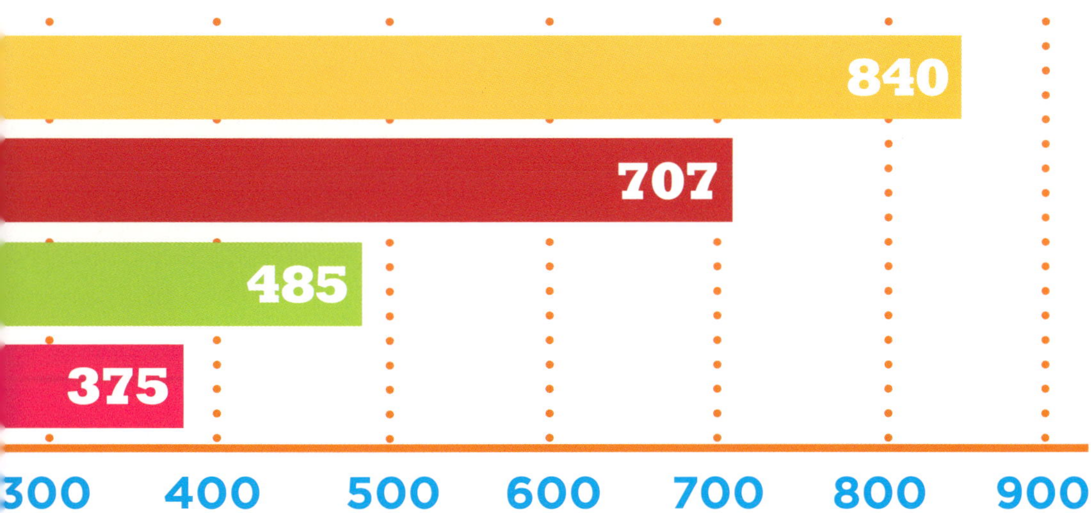

PARTS OF A HELLCAT

HOOD SCOOP
HEADLIGHTS
SRT
GRILLE

CHAPTER 2

Design

Drivers love the Hellcat's looks. Its large body is square. It has four round headlights. The taillights are rectangular. They give the car a unique look as it races by.

Two of the headlights are hollow. They let more air move to the engine. The air helps cool the engine.

SQUARE BODY
SRT

ROUND HEADLIGHTS
SRT

RECTANGULAR
TAILLIGHTS
SRT
DODGE
SRT

Inside the Hellcat

Inside, a thick steering wheel greets the driver. He or she can use a touch screen for navigation. It acts as a backup camera too. The seats are heated. They're also cooled. Some buyers get their Hellcats with sunroofs.

The Hellcat comes with two keys. The red key lets the car use all of its power. The black key limits power.

Colors and Stripes

Hellcats come in several colors. Buyers can also add stripes. Stripes make the car look even more intimidating. Some people want an even tougher look. They order all-black hoods.

SRT

MANY OPTIONS

Buyers have many options.

12
EXTERIOR COLORS

3
SEAT COLORS

4 BRAKE CALIPER COLORS

3 WHEEL OPTIONS

The Widebody

For some drivers, bigger is always better. The Widebody option is for them. It is 3.5 inches (9 centimeters) wider than normal. It has wider wheels too. They need **fender** flares.

The standard Hellcat has 9.5-inch (24-cm) tires. The Widebody's are 1.5 inches (4 cm) wider. Wider tires give the car more grip. More grip makes turning and stopping easier.

SRT

CHAPTER 3

Power and Performance

Using touch screens, drivers can change settings. They can pick driving modes. They decide how the car handles. With certain settings, the Hellcat tears up the strip. With others, it's perfect for daily drives.

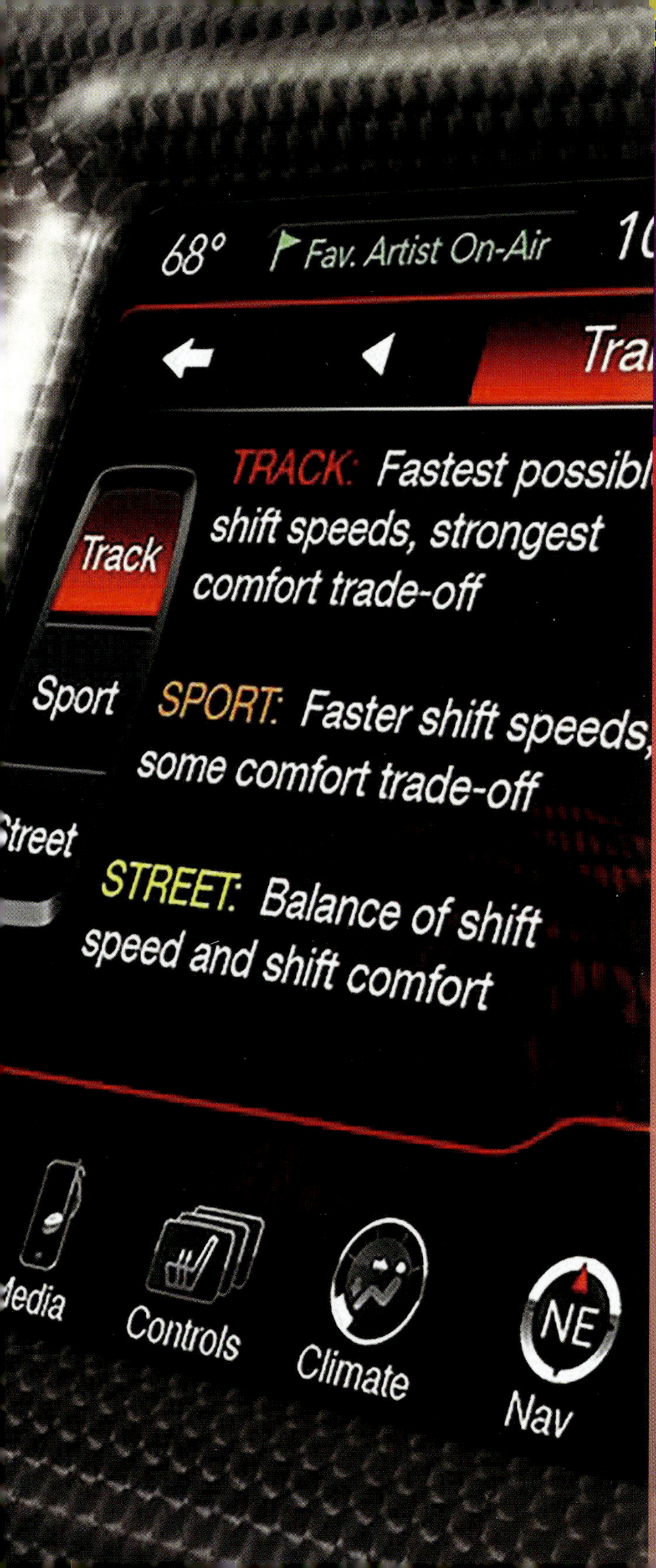

DRIVING MODES

CUSTOM
made up of saved settings

STREET
best for daily driving

ECO
uses less gas

SPORT
best for sporty driving

TRACK
best for smooth tracks

VALET
limits power

Most Hellcats come with manual transmissions. Drivers shift gears themselves.